NATIONAL
GEOGRAPHIC

Flags

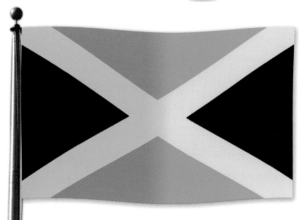

Jan Pritchett

Look at this flag.
It has one circle.

This flag has two squares.

This flag has three rectangles.

This flag has four triangles.

This flag has five stars.

This flag has six stripes.

This flag has lots of stars and stripes!